Kennedy/Reagan

*An Imaginary Talk
Given by
Senator Edward Moore Kennedy
And
President Ronald Wilson Reagan*

A Play by John C. Kendall

*Based on the lives and words of
Senator Edward Kennedy
and
President Ronald Reagan*

ISBN: 1484817273

ISBN-13: 978-1484817278

Back cover photo by Chris Macke.

Dedicated to

the memory of

Senator Edward Moore Kennedy

and

President Ronald Wilson Reagan,

two great American statesmen.

CHARACTERS

Host
Senator Edward Moore Kennedy
President Ronald Wilson Reagan

SCENE

If both Kennedy and Reagan are played by the same actor one podium is placed center stage, accompanied by an American flag prominently displayed on stage.

If two actors play the roles of Kennedy and Reagan respectively, then two podiums will be needed. House lights remain up giving the aura of a formal meeting, allowing performers to see the audience. Note: HOST can be played by the same actor that portrays Kennedy and Reagan or by another actor.

HOST
(*Enters to podium and addresses audience.*)
Welcome everyone to this momentous occasion. Thank you all for coming. I am honored to introduce to you President Ronald Wilson Reagan. I am also honored to introduce Senator Edward Moore Kennedy of Massachusetts.
        (*As Kennedy and Reagan enter they wave to the audience as they take their place at respective podiums.*)
Mr. President and Senator we are honored that you are here and thank you for coming.

REAGAN
Hello and thank you for the invitation.

KENNEDY

I'd like to thank you all for inviting me and for being here as well.

HOST

Gentleman, we are anxious for both of you to discuss your lives and give us some of your inspiring words. We will now turn the floor over to both of you.

(Host exits the stage.)

REAGAN

I'd like to start off with excerpts from a speech that marked a real turning point in my life.

My fellow Americans, I've spent most of my life as a Democrat. I recently have seen fit to follow another course. I believe that the issues confronting us cross party lines. Now, one side in this campaign has been telling us that the issues of this election are the maintenance of peace and prosperity. The line has been used, "We've never had it so good!" But I have, and I'm comfortable feeling that this prosperity isn't something upon which we can base our hopes for the future. No nation in history has ever survived a tax burden that reached a third of its national income. Today, thirty-seven cents out of every dollar earned in this country is the tax collector's share, and yet our government continues to spend seventeen million dollars a day more than the government takes in.

In this vote-harvesting time they use terms like the "Great Society", or as we were told a few days ago by the president, we must accept a "greater government activity in the affairs of the people". I'd like to remind you of three words that begin the Constitution of the United States: "We the people...".

You and I have a rendezvous with destiny. We will preserve for our children this, the last best hope of man on earth, or we will sentence them to take the last step into a thousand years of darkness. You and I have the ability and the dignity and the right to make our own decisions and determine our own destiny.

KENNEDY

Well, Ron, that was a beautiful speech you made for Goldwater in '64. I think that really did launch your political career. But the only problem was that I think your Republican buddies liked you so much that they realized at that point, that they had nominated the wrong candidate for president. It may have worked against Barry because it showed the personal power that you had. Barry was well liked at the time by Republicans but you wowed them with that speech. Oh well, you know what they say, "the cream rises to the top".

REAGAN

Thank you, Ted. Now I'm interested in hearing, and I'm sure the audience is interested as well, when you first realized that you were indeed a real contender for public office.

KENNEDY

After Jack's election as president, Bobby and I needed a break so we went on a trip to Acapulco. Bobby confided in me that he didn't plan to seek the Senate seat that Jack vacated in '60. The seat was held at the time by a fellow named Ben Smith. He had been appointed by Gov. Foster Furcolo to finish out Jack's term. He'd been Jack's Harvard roommate. I heard that Ben agreed to hold on to the seat until I turned thirty, the legal age to be a U.S. Senator. By law the governor was permitted to appoint someone to fill the senate vacancy for two years until the next scheduled federal election in '62 which just so happened to be the year I turned thirty. Whoever would win that election would fill the remaining two years of Jack's six-year term. After that the winner could run for the full six year term. I questioned my own inexperience. I thought that people would see me as simply a beneficiary of my family's political power. All of my life I felt that I wanted to "catch up" with the rest of my family. On Sunday, March 11, 1962, I went on the news show *Meet the Press*, a few days prior to announcing my candidacy for the U.S. Senate. I discussed that my family had always impressed upon my brothers and myself the importance of public service and being involved in public affairs. I explained that to me there is "no occupation that is more interesting, more stimulating, and if done well more rewarding than public service".

REAGAN

Well Ted, I certainly must commend you on your call to public service. You certainly could have just taken it easy and enjoyed a life of ease based on your family's wealth. But something in your heart, soul, and mind told you that in biblical terms, "To whom much is given, much is expected." I on the other hand, wasn't born of privilege and had to "work my way up" as they say but I don't begrudge you the fact that you were privileged. However, I applaud you for using your advanced standing for unselfish reasons giving of your time and efforts to help the people of the nation as you saw fit to do.

The joy of involvement in making a better world was expressed by me as far back as my high school days. I'm quoted in my high school yearbook as saying "Life is just one grand sweet song, so start the music." Only trouble is my name is spelled wrong in the yearbook. That quote is attributed to Donald Reagan.

Although Ted, life is a sweet song I understand and respect the fact that you stayed in public life even though your family suffered many great tragedies.

KENNEDY

Yes, after my brother Jack was assassinated it changed my family; it changed the United States and the history of the world. Mostly everybody at some point has wondered how life would have been had Jack not been killed. The nation and indeed the world would have, I'm sure, been a better place. The same can be said for when Bobby was killed. After that, all attention fell upon me. Could I uphold the family standing and leadership? I was thought of as the last heir to Camelot. With that came a lot of pressure. Pressure to make good on the hope and the dream, and the promise to lead our nation and the world into that idealized notion of Camelot, the perfect time and place.

Ron, you had a challenging time yourself with an assassination attempt against you as well and like a true star, you made a miraculous comeback.

REAGAN

Let's talk about that later. For now I'd like to lighten things up.

KENNEDY

Ron, I always found it interesting how you were described by some people in the media as the "Great Communicator" and also at the same time as the "Rodney Dangerfield of

Politics". They said you can't get any respect. You were constantly criticized for not coming up with any of your own ideas. It was said that you had a scripted presidency. Personally I think you were on the right track in the very beginning of your career when you were a liberal Democrat. I know that your die hard conservative buddies want to push that under the rug, but you were a Democrat. When you first started out the establishment wouldn't take you seriously because you were an actor instead of a lawyer or businessman. It was joked, and not nicely so, that you were a fading movie actor upstaged by a chimpanzee in Bedtime for Bonzo. They painted you as a thespian simply reciting lines written by someone else without any true convictions of your own. I have to hand it to you Ron, you showed them all and you trounced the Democrats at times.

REAGAN
I worked on the mission of helping people to achieve self-reliance.

KENNEDY
Ron, you are a sharp Republican. During your years as president you never talked about cutting Social Security and Medicare for people who were currently dependent on those programs. Even though you professed strongly the Republican mantra of "trickle down economics" you were careful not to isolate voters by scaring them. You really used the whole tax cut thing to your advantage. That's why we Dems couldn't gain any headway against you. You didn't appear to be, even to many of the Dems, the typical Republican ogre who would usually talk about reducing Social Security and Medicare. You had us "on the ropes"

Ron. The presidency turned out to be your role of a lifetime and you played it to the hilt.

I'll admit it Ron, you definitely have a star quality about you. No wonder Nancy fell for you as much as most of the American people did.

REAGAN

Flattery will get you everywhere Ted. When I first announced my candidacy for the Republican nomination for President at the New York Hilton on November 13, 1979, I believe that I touched a nerve in the American people. Americans were suffering from a "crisis of confidence that strikes at the very heart and soul and spirit of our national will". I spoke about the principles of self-reliance, self-discipline, morality and, above all, responsible liberty for every individual.

I talked about setting a new agenda for the United States. Here are some key elements of that speech:

No problem that we face today can compare with the need to restore the health of the American economy and the strength of the American dollar.

Double-digit inflation has robbed you and your family of the ability to plan. It has destroyed the confidence to buy and it threatens the very structure of family itself as more and more wives are forced to work in order to help meet the ever-increasing cost of living. At the same time, the lack of real growth in the economy has introduced the justifiable fear in the minds of working men and women who are already overextended that soon there will be fewer jobs and no money to pay for even the necessities of life. And tragically as the cost of living keeps going up, the standard of living, which has been our great pride, keeps going down.

The federal government has overspent, overestimated, and over-regulated. It has failed to deliver services within the revenues it should be allowed to raise from taxes.

You and I pay taxes imposed on business every time we go to the store. Only people pay taxes and it is political demagoguery or economic illiteracy to try and tell us otherwise.

By reducing federal tax rates where they discourage individual initiative-especially personal income tax rates- we can restore incentives, invite greater economic growth and at the same time help give us better government instead of bigger government.

In short, a punitive tax system must be replaced by one that restores incentive for the worker and for industry; a system that rewards initiative and effort and encourages thrift.

KENNEDY

Ron, I know you're all worked up here. But just as an aside to you mentioning women working, I can't believe that when you spoke in 1979, you still made the point about women staying home and not having a career. You know Ron, women are equals and need to reach their full potential.

REAGAN

I know you're pulling my leg Ted, but it was back in 1979 you know.

KENNEDY

I guess it took you a few years to catch up, huh? Just having fun Ron.

Sincerely Ron, you and my brother, Jack, had a lot in common, although you were on opposite sides of the political river. You both charmed America with your big

11

smiles and a sort of Walt Disney optimism which expressed that almost anything was possible in the United States based on the inherent good will of the majority of our citizens. My brother launched the space race which succeeded in the United States putting men on the moon, and you solved the problem of the Cold War.

REAGAN

Well Ted, as I had stated in one of my speeches, America is great because America is good. In my 1981 Inaugural Address I discussed that those who say that we're in a time when there are no heroes, they just don't know where to look. You can see heroes every day going in and out of factory gates. Others, a handful in number, produce enough food to feed all of us and then the world beyond. You meet heroes across a counter – and they're on both sides of that counter. There are entrepreneurs – with faith in themselves and faith in an idea – who create new jobs, new wealth and opportunity. They're individuals and families whose taxes support the government and whose voluntary gifts support church, charity, culture, art, and education. Their patriotism is quiet, but deep. Their values sustain our national life.

KENNEDY

Ron, that certainly was beautiful, and I agree but, I think that sometimes it was necessary to help those American heroes along with good, tangible government policy. After the assassination of Jack, I worked very closely with President Johnson on passing the Civil Rights Bill which Jack had fought for. We Democrats at the time were pushing for everything that you Republicans would later try to reverse. LBJ moved along many programs which were not only his own but also conceived by Jack and Bobby; Most notably was The War on Poverty, The Economic Opportunity Act which included The Job Corps and Project Head Start, Medicare, Medicaid, The National Endowment for the Arts and Humanities, Vista, and others.

I love you Ron, but your take on government was the epitome of laissez-faire. I believe in the "take the bull by the horns" action approach.

REAGAN

But those are all giveaway programs Ted. After I became a Republican, I realized that we needed to show people that the best way to advance in society is to learn how to do an "honest days work for an honest days pay". Taking from those who are working hard to give to those who aren't is an example of societal decay. It's no wonder that the deficit is so high. You've created a society where large numbers of people don't know how to earn a living. Not by their own fault mind you, but by the fault of liberals who thought that they were doing good works of charity and mercy. Government can't solve everyone's problems. Government is the problem. We have a huge deficit, not because we tax too little, but rather that we spend too much. You see Ted, as the old saying has it, "give a man a fish and you feed him for a day, teach him how to fish and you feed him for his entire life".

KENNEDY

Yes, but there has to be enough fish in his part of the ocean and he can't have a leaky boat.

REAGAN

Ted, it doesn't work if we overtax the very people who will invest in America and create jobs.

KENNEDY

They have enough to spare. You speak to support the notion that the rich are entitled <u>not</u> to help those that are less fortunate. May I remind you Ron that God gave this world to <u>all</u> of his people. Just because someone's ancestors got to our shores earlier and claimed a lot of land or inherited resources, that doesn't mean that they are exonerated from any obligation to make America better by helping each other. Where is the morality in the so-called moral majority? I understand that we need wealthy people and corporations to invest in creating jobs and supposedly, to use words from members of your party, the wealth will "trickle down" to the working class and poor. However, that scenario doesn't work and the wealth doesn't usually trickle very quickly or steadily. Government sometimes needs to help the money move a little faster than a trickle. Your own Vice President George H. W. Bush called your economic plan "voodoo economics" when he was running against you for the nomination for President.

REAGAN

Well, it took him a little while to catch on, but I convinced him.

What still really bothers me is that some Americans don't have a true sense of what the United States really stands for – how blessed and lucky they are just to have been born in this great land. Some apathetic people just go about their everyday lives and don't even bother to vote. Many nations of the world are still ruled by dictators. To this day, in some areas of the world people are still not free. Authors cannot publish their books without censorship, or at all. People cannot choose a career path or refuse one and who they associate with or not is dictated to them. There is still a long

14

way to go. We must keep the task of creating total world freedom alive.

The signing of the Declaration of Independence in Philadelphia, in 1776, has been described as a miracle. I truly believe that it was a miracle and that God sent his heavenly power down that day when the USA was born.

KENNEDY

Amen, I agree with you there Ron.

REAGAN

Ted, I want to talk for a moment about a really interesting experience I had in May of 1988 when I was in Moscow to sign formal ratification papers for the INF Treaty. There I was at Moscow State University, standing in front of a huge statue of Lenin. I addressed some of the Soviet Union's future leaders. At that time, the evil empire hadn't fallen yet. Well, I told them about the blessings of freedom, democracy and free enterprise. They loved it! I had them in the palm of my hand with Lenin's philosophy symbolically behind me as almost a sort of "sign off" to the old gentleman and his worn out, failed doctrine.

KENNEDY

Ron, I'm sure Kennedy family members smiled up in heaven as the Berlin Wall was torn down.

REAGAN

Ted, I know your family has had more than your fair share of trials and horrible tragedies.

KENNEDY

People generally feel a closeness to my family because we were so much a part of their lives. That's why in a special way, to honor Joe, Jack, Bobby, and John-John, I continue the fight to keep the dream alive in standing up for those people who can't stand up for themselves.

It was wonderful growing up together, mostly in Hyannis Port. My family has always had a great deal of love for the sea. We're all sailors to a degree. While my brother was president, he would often sit on the front porch in Hyannis Port and gaze into the ocean and that would help him to clear his mind. Suddenly a great problem would be made clear. I enjoyed many hours on my boat as John did on his. The sea is calming and life-restoring. Much of this of course was due to my father purchasing the family compound by the sea in Hyannis Port. You know, I've painted pictures of my sailboat. Painting has also given me peace, and it also served to give me great relaxation.

REAGAN

To me the ultimate relaxation always came from horseback riding with the sound of the hooves, squeak of the leather, sun on your head, and smell of the horse and saddle, with trees around – things just naturally straighten out in my mind. I learned to ride horses back in Dixon, Illinois where I grew up. During summers in my high school and college years I worked as a lifeguard at a local swimming park. On days when the swimming section was empty I was allowed to ride the manager's horse. I didn't have an ocean nearby Ted, but the Rock River gave me plenty of time in its waters. In seven years as a lifeguard I can proudly say that I saved seventy-seven people from drowning.

KENNEDY

That's very impressive Ron. You must have been the best lifeguard they ever had. Are you sure that it wasn't because you were so handsome that the girls pretended they were drowning? I'd like to reminisce a little about my childhood as well. My father always made sure that our family got together frequently and always made sure that we talked politics. The entire family would be included in discussing how to solve some major problem in the country or the world. We had many friends; but most importantly we were friends to each other and we always helped and supported each other. Our dad made sure that we children never showed off our wealth. He wouldn't buy us a bicycle or a car until others in our peer group had gotten theirs first. Dad wanted us to distinguish our reputation through good deeds rather than exploiting our family's wealth, an excellent lesson that we've all tried to live by.

Now for the benefit of the audience, I'd like to get back to touching on some social issues. Let's take retirement for example. Most working people dream of that wonderful time of retirement when they can finally wake up in the morning and do what they want to do. For the vast majority of Americans, retirement means freedom and happiness. This was made possible of course by the Democrats in FDR's time, under his leadership in creating Social Security. Medicare was brought about by President Lyndon Johnson. Remember however, without my brother Jack, there may not have been a President Johnson. Thus, no Medicare or a War on Poverty.

REAGAN

You know Ted, life without some kind of work is awfully boring. I'd just like to relate another story. I have a friend who told me that in the small town where he lives, there is a library dedicated to a man who was once the mayor of the town, as well as an extremely successful entrepreneur and philanthropist. The people of the town loved him so much that after he passed on they placed the man's desk in the library as a tribute. On the desk is a rectangular box with the words: 'The Secret of Success' engraved on top. When one opens the box, one word is inscribed inside followed by an exclamation mark. That word is WORK!

Sometimes the social programs encourage able-bodied people to be, I don't mean this cruelly, to be freeloaders and to live off of other hard-working taxpayers. I'm not talking about the truly needy; I'm just talking about people who can work.

Many Democrats were in my corner, you know, the "Reagan Democrats". That's how I won election and re-election to the presidency. Obviously, with more voters registered as Democrats than Republicans, I couldn't have won without a lot of Democrat votes. Back in the malaise days of President Jimmy Carter I was able to bring hope to not only Republicans but also Democrats who had given up all hope that America would ever progress again. During the campaign at Liberty State Park in New Jersey on Labor Day, September 1, 1980, I believe my speech gave our citizens hope again as Lady Liberty stood there shining light from her great torch of hope. It was a time of economic recession. The following three sentences of my speech brought the most applause:

A recession is defined as when your neighbor loses his job. A depression is when you lose your job. Recovery is when Jimmy Carter loses his job.

KENNEDY

I remember you created a lot of buzz with that speech Ron. You really hit President Carter with a one-two punch there. And I don't think he ever recovered. Indeed, I think you, my brothers, and FDR were probably the best American speech-makers in my lifetime. I'll say you truly earned the title of "The Great Communicator". Much of it, of course, is attributed to your acting ability. Even one of our best Dems, the great House Speaker Tip O'Neill, who by the way didn't agree with you on anything regarding public policy, admitted no one could hold a candle to you in public speaking. One of your best speeches, which Tip mentioned, was made on the day of the horribly unfortunate disaster when the space shuttle Challenger exploded just after liftoff. You quoted a World War II Royal Canadian Air Force Pilot, John Gillespie Magee, Jr., a poet who was killed in action. Ron, I'm sure we'd all like to hear again that famous line that you delivered in your speech honoring the Challenger astronauts on January 28, 1986.

REAGAN

The crew of the space shuttle Challenger honored us by the manner in which they lived their lives. We will never forget them, nor the last time we saw them this morning, as they prepared for their journey and waved goodbye and "slipped the surly bonds of earth to touch the face of God".

KENNEDY

After that Tip O'Neill expressed what I think most Americans were thinking when he said about you, "He's the best public speaker I've ever seen".

REAGAN

Thank you, Ted. You of course are also a great speaker.

KENNEDY

Flattery will get you everywhere, but for the benefit of the audience, I figure it might be good to get back to some issues. Let's discuss economic policy. Ron, you believe in governing by tax cuts. That was one of the major disagreements we had while we served at the same time. You think that tax cuts will make everything okay. I completely understand that we can't kill people with taxes, but the concept of the wealthy paying their fair share is what makes the United States different from the old royal and feudal societies, where groups of people were divided into the elite on top and the peasants on the bottom. Tax cuts are not a cure all for everything. What guarantee is there that the wealthy, upon saving large sums of money, will use any of it to help those less fortunate? Why would they not just let it sit in their bank account in order to simply feather their own nest?

REAGAN

Well, if the wealthy are taxed too much, what incentive will there be for anyone to work hard to achieve wealth? Ted, I think that my administration proved that cutting taxes along with a few other adjustments will cause the economy to boom. That's what the whole so-called "Reagan Revolution" was all about. As I'm sure that you remember the malaise and stagflation of the years of the Carter Administration was destroying the possibility of many Americans to achieve "The American Dream". The story of my economic plan, which was referred to as Supply-side Economics or as some said Reaganomics, went like this:

First, we reduced both the size and role of the Federal Government. Domestic Policy agenda focused on cutting taxes, balancing the budget, reducing the cost of social welfare programs, and returning some powers to State Governments. Once we began to accomplish these goals, the Federal Government saved billions of dollars and stimulated the economy at the same time.

KENNEDY

Ron the problem with Reaganomics was that it didn't stimulate the personal economies of people in need. Man does not live by tax cuts alone.

REAGAN

There he goes again. I believe that the record speaks for itself. My administration's tax and spending cuts brought about the largest peace time expansion in our nation's history. Jobs need to be created by the private sector. Government spending is a drag on consumer spending. If people's money is taken in taxes then they can't buy things and job creation is stagnant. Entrepreneurs need capital to invest in scientists to utilize their brain power for new inventions and research and development to produce new products and services.

KENNEDY

We need to spend more money on education and job training.

REAGAN

The only problem Ted is what jobs will we train people to do? Without government getting out of the way to allow businesses to thrive, there won't be any new jobs created.

In the late 70's high marginal tax rates were adversely affecting economic output. Tax cuts were necessary to spur the economy. My administration led the way to lower income tax and capital gains tax rates while lifting many cumbersome regulations on businesses. I lowered barriers for business people to produce goods and services. American consumers benefitted from a greater supply of goods and services at lower prices. Furthermore, I reduced the growth of the Federal Government and cut unnecessary government spending. As a result, the economy did better than it had in years. We left the recession behind and started a long period of economic growth. While some called the plan Reaganomics, my name for it is common sense. You see Ted, if job producers are taxed at too high of a rate, what incentive will they have to produce new jobs; therefore what good will they be for anyone else who is looking for a job? The burden of taxation robs our society of rewards which encourage accomplishment: such as making profits to reinvest and hire people. My administration made citizens feel that it was "Morning in America" again, as my campaign advertisement said. We made people feel a sense of positive anticipation, like a new day was dawning, and that everyone would feel good again, with plenty of hope for the future – that something wonderful was coming right around the corner. The Reagan years in the White House made our citizens remember that America is like a "Shining city on a hill", the "Last, best hope for mankind on earth".

Citizens became, once again, proud of the United States of America.

KENNEDY
Ron, I remind you however, that as New York Governor Mario Cuomo pointed out, there were still a great deal of tarnishes on the shining city. Not every part of the city was brilliant. There was still unemployment and individuals who could not support themselves. There were still people who could not afford basic healthcare. Some people fell through the cracks in the shining metal.

REAGAN
I was criticized for not giving some people everything that they thought they wanted. It was true that I could pick up the Sunday newspaper on any given week and look at hundreds of jobs listed and wonder why the people who are complaining about being unemployed don't apply for those jobs. I know that view is simplistic, and not everyone is a perfect match for jobs listed in the want ads. But still it always seemed that there were many entry level jobs that unemployed people could perform rather than collecting unemployment benefits and complaining that no jobs are available for them. My father sold shoes and my mother worked as a seamstress when possible to put bread on the table. Sometimes taking on a small job can lead to a bigger one. While I was governor of California, we had a program to match welfare recipients with jobs.

KENNEDY
As I learned though Ron, it didn't work all that well because most of the jobs that you matched people with required a higher level of education and skills than those people had,

and therefore they didn't last long on the job. You can't just throw people to work without proper training.

REAGAN

Some were very successful Ted and stayed in the workforce.

KENNEDY

Well I think most did not. I beg to differ. You can't just throw a person into a job without proper training and support. With the capitalistic system, which by the way I do endorse, there will always be individuals who need help. Business cycles go up and down. We of course ideally want them to stay up but in reality we need to always have a safety net for the less fortunate people among us, for example, persons with disabilities, persons who don't have the education credentials or skills needed for filling particular jobs. There are women raising children alone and can't work because there is no one home to take care of the children. Those of us who are fortunate enough to have health and the means to take care of ourselves and our families need to help those who cannot. Of course that means keeping up Social Security, Medicare, Medicaid, Welfare, Unemployment Insurance, and one of the major causes of my life quality, affordable, healthcare for all Americans. Every American should have the opportunity to receive a quality education, a job that respects their dignity and protects their safety, and healthcare that does not condemn those whose health is impaired to a lifetime of poverty and lost opportunity.

Jack wanted to eliminate the problem of people not having decent quality healthcare. He began to work on Medicare before he was killed. Then LBJ, to his credit, finished the job and signed Medicare into law in 1965. The disgrace is that we still do not have sufficient, fair, quality, affordable health care for all citizens.

REAGAN

Ted, I think we know where we stand on those major issues and I'm sure we'll get back to those, but while I'm standing here with Camelot's last brother I'd like to express, as many Americans have over the years, the following questions:
First, what if Lee Harvey Oswald never fired a shot in Dallas? What would the world have been like? Second, if Sirhan Sirhan didn't fire that shot in Los Angeles, what would the world have been like? And finally, if the accident at Chappaquiddick hadn't occurred what would the world have been like?

KENNEDY

Thank God you were not injured in the assassination attempt against you.

REAGAN

I truly believe that God protected me. It just wasn't my time yet. There was still so much to do. I was barely two months into my presidency. Once I realized what had happened, that I'd been shot, I knew that somehow I was going to pull through. After arriving at the hospital, the first thing I thought of was to calm Nancy down, I thought that a joke would do the trick. I said, "Nancy I forgot to duck." Then as I was going into surgery I made sure that I said to the team of doctors, "I hope you're all Republicans". Later after starting to recover, when I was told who shot me, I made it clear that I was hoping it was the KGB. But then I said, "On second thought, they wouldn't have missed!"

KENNEDY

You know, regarding that question of "What would the world have been like if...?" Looking back on President Nixon's time, when then Vice President Spiro Agnew resigned, you were one of the people being considered by President Nixon to become Vice President, along with Nelson Rockefeller, John Connolly, and Gerald Ford. If you had been asked would you have taken the job?

REAGAN

Well I guess I'll never really know the answer.

KENNEDY

It's sort of intriguing to think about that because you would have become president much earlier and under different circumstances. If it had been you, would you have pardoned Nixon or not? We'll never know if you would have been elected for a full term on your own.

REAGAN

Ted, I guess we're members of the 'What if?' club. We're part of that small group of individuals who have been critically involved with the top echelons of US Government that were affected by fate enough to make historians ponder the 'What if?' factor. In 1980, I got a chance to pull the nation forward. The American people need quality leadership. They need a president who can lift their hopes and help them fulfill their dreams. They need a president to encourage entrepreneurs by having government step out of the way and take away unnecessary outdated regulations which hamper creativity and growth. The president must lead the way to make sure that the Federal Government doesn't grow too big and that more local issues be handled by state and local governments. For example, the Federal Government should be concerned with supporting the military, not fixing potholes. The president needs to create the environment of a "can do" attitude. Citizens need to feel that in America there is every opportunity for success and no opportunity for failure.

I know of a man who was born with a severe disability. This gentleman has a great deal of difficulty walking and speaking but still he goes to work everyday at the local supermarket. He qualifies for much government support, but rather than sitting at home he walks to the local supermarket and performs a job, makes wages, and gives back to the economy. His example should set the tone for all of us. A person is only down on their luck if they will themselves to be that way. President Franklin Roosevelt helped to lead the nation out of the Great Depression when he said, "The only thing we have to fear is fear itself." As a young man listening to the radio FDR inspired me to have drive, ambition, and to make something of myself and to help others to help themselves. Americans need to feel that they are leaders. It's my belief that God had a divine plan that placed this great continent between two oceans to be sought out by those who have an abiding love of freedom and a special kind of courage.

KENNEDY

Ron, sometimes talk is not enough. For example, when Bobby ran for the presidency he was bothered by the deterioration of our cities. He saw needless poverty, decay and violence. He saw homelessness, people in despair and angry, racial prejudice, as well as American lives and millions and millions of dollars being spent in Vietnam on a war which was wrongly entered into and fought. Bobby

27

saw war dollars being spent while programs that helped economic opportunity were being cut back. When Bobby made his announcement to run for president he said, "I do not run to oppose any man, but to propose new policies". At the funeral mass for Bobby at St. Patrick's Cathedral in Manhattan, I read one of Bobby's speeches in which he acknowledged evils of the world such as slavery, slaughter, starvation and repression but then said "that those who live with us are our brothers; that they share with us the same short moment of life; that they seek – as we do – nothing but the chance to live out their lives in purpose and happiness...surely this bond of common faith, this bond of common good, can begin to teach us something". Then I added for my brother to be remembered as a good and decent man, who saw wrong and tried to right it, saw suffering and tried to heal it, saw war and tried to stop it. Those of us who loved him and who take him to his rest today pray that what he was to us and what he wished for others will someday come to pass for all the world. As he said many times in paraphrasing George Bernard Shaw, in many parts of this nation to those he touched and who sought to touch him, "Some men see things as they are and say why. I dream things that never were and say why not."

REAGAN

That was a beautiful eulogy Ted. Not only did you comfort your family, but the rest of us who felt the loss of Bobby. I'm sure that soon after you began to feel the pressure of being the last Kennedy brother and what that would mean.

KENNEDY

It's true. Less than an hour after Bobby's death, people who were distraught, disappointed and desperate to regain the hope, implored me to move stronger into the nation's politics. I was told that I was all that the Democratic Party had left. Hubert Humphrey asked me to run on his ticket as the vice presidential candidate. But it was too much, too soon. I didn't feel that I was ready yet.

REAGAN

It took me awhile to decide to run as well. Like you, with Democrats, I was urged to enter politics by people in the Republican Party who were desperately in search of someone who could show strong leadership and win over the voters. To go back to the very beginning, the thought of being president first struck me upon my graduation from Eureka College, back in Illinois, when the college president handed me my diploma and asked, "Are you better off today than you were four years ago?" Later as you know I used that line in the Presidential Campaign Debate against President Jimmy Carter. I think that line alone may have won me the presidency. The other great line I used just popped into my head when President Carter made a statement that I was against Social Security and Medicare. Feeling in my gut that his statement was false I blurted out "There he goes again". That single debate probably changed the history of the world.

As you know, before entering politics, I was very happy as a motion picture actor and television personality. For my entire life, until the beginning of the 1960's, I was a Democrat. I grew up listening to FDR's Fireside Chats and my parents idolized him. I was a labor leader and president of the Screen Actor's Guild.

After World War II, there was a definite Communist effort to infiltrate the movie business and in effect, control the hearts and minds of American citizens. I fought against the

29

Communists. There was a national backlash against Hollywood. Politicians attacked the movie industry as harboring "Reds" and immoral people. Organizations around the country began pushing for the censoring of movies. As president of SAG, I thought it best to speak out in defense of our industry. At first, I spoke to Hollywood insiders and theater owners hoping to inspire them to improve the image of the industry by standing up for the truth against unfair accusations. Soon as I was giving more and more speeches, I spread out to groups outside the industry such as The Rotary and Chambers of Commerce. That's when I feel that my political transformation began. As stated prior, I had always been a Democrat and considered myself a liberal. I mistrusted business and believed that government could solve all of the nation's problems as it did to bring us out of the Great Depression. Later I came to realize that World War II probably did more to end the Depression than government intervention.

KENNEDY

I beg to differ with you there Ron. FDR and his administration were the saviors of democracy and freedom. Roosevelt's bold actions kept the country from turning towards Communism at a time when people were starving.

REAGAN

There he goes again.

KENNEDY

Excuse me; I'll let you finish your story.

REAGAN

Well, I think my political change from Dem to Republican began during the war when I witnessed many Civil Service bureaucrats work with a lazy "business as usual" attitude performing redundant tasks. Then I spent some time in England working on a picture called "The Hasty Heart". At that time, the Labor Party was in power. I got a first hand look at how their "welfare state" policies drained people's incentive to work. I meditated on the words of the founder of the Democratic Party, Thomas Jefferson, and of course Ted, I knew Thomas Jefferson. I worked with Thomas Jefferson. Thomas Jefferson was a friend of mine and he said that "the best government is the smallest government". He also said, "Governments are not the masters of the people, but the servants of the people governed."

During the Depression, the Democrats created a massive government bureaucracy which began to plan and regulate the economic and social lives of our citizens and intruded in areas best left to private enterprise. I became upset with seeing how politicians with the best of intentions were leading America towards socialism. They were confiscating a disproportionate share of the nation's wealth through excessive taxation and were in effect controlling day to day management of businesses with stringent rules and regulations. As a well known movie personality, I fell into the ninety-four percent income tax bracket. Ninety-four percent of every dollar I earned was taken away from my family. Where is the fairness in that? That's about when I formed my own government principal: There probably isn't any undertaking on earth, short of assuring the national security, that can't be handled more efficiently by the forces of private enterprise than by the federal government.

KENNEDY

But Ron, try telling that to all of those who would be completely penniless without Social Security or who would die without Medicare.

REAGAN

There he goes again.

KENNEDY

Sorry again Ron, you have the floor.

REAGAN

In 1954, I started performing in GE Theater on TV. I acted occasionally but every week I hosted the show. As part of my work for GE I traveled to GE plants around the country and continued making speeches.

In 1960, I officially turned from liberal Democrat to Republican. It was the year when Richard Nixon ran against your brother Ted. I said to Nancy, you know, something just dawned on me; all these things I've been saying about government getting too big...well, it just came to me that I'm supporting political candidates who are responsible for the things I'm criticizing. So far, I'd been working for just about any Democrat who would accept my help. I even urged Dwight Eisenhower to run for president as a Democrat. When Ike decided to run as a Republican, I decided: If I truly considered him the best man for the job, he still ought to be my choice. So, I campaigned and voted for Ike, my first for a Republican. I volunteered to register as a Republican and campaign for Nixon against your brother. When I told Nixon that I was going to change my party affiliation to Republican, he said I'd be more effective if I campaigned as a Democrat, so I agreed to wait until after the election to change my party affiliation. After your father heard about my decision Ted, he tried to persuade me to change my mind and support your brother, but I turned him down.

KENNEDY

Big mistake Ron. You should have done what my Dad asked. You may have been president earlier and we wouldn't have had Watergate.

REAGAN

An interesting thought, but on with the story as it happened… So, even though I agreed to Nixon's request, I really was no longer a Democrat by 1960. In 1962, while again campaigning for Nixon in his attempt to unseat California's Democratic governor, the tax-and-spend liberal Pat Brown, I made it official: During one of my speeches a woman stood up and asked me if I'd registered as a Republican yet. I said I hadn't yet, but I intended to. Then she said that she was a registrar and walked up and placed a registration form in front of me. I signed it and became an official Republican at that moment.

KENNEDY

Oh so now we know, that's when you turned to the dark side.

REAGAN

We'll talk about Star Wars later Ted. Well, the speech that I started out with, way at the beginning of our discussion, the 1964 speech for Barry Goldwater; that was what really got me a lot of national attention. After that national broadcast on October 27 of '64, I was not only known as a movie and television personality, but also as a strong political influence. The following spring, a group of businessmen asked if they could convince me to run for governor of California. Finally I agreed to do it.

KENNEDY

Gee, I'm glad it was a lot easier for me to choose my party affiliation. I was born a Democrat and always remained one. No offense Ron, but I always thought that a person who could change parties, couldn't be trusted.

REAGAN

I've stated publicly, it wasn't that I left them but rather, they changed and left me. It was a fever of big government programs, I admit, brought on by the Great Depression. But overkill is overkill.

KENNEDY

Again, not meaning any insult here, but party loyalty is something that I cherish. Without party loyalty, what have you got except politicians "blowing with the wind" and little getting done? Who can you rely on when you need votes to get a bill passed? Who can you rely on when you need support and the chips are down? I think it's infinitely better to work within the party to get your point across and then work for change in platform or policy with party members who at least think alike on most issues.

REAGAN

Great minds think for themselves. When I was elected governor of California, I got the chance to put everything I'd been preaching about into practice. Much of what was accomplished in California, I later repeated on the national scale as president. I announced my candidacy for president on November 13, 1979, at the New York Hilton. Some of it went like this: Someone once said that the difference between an American and any other kind of person is that an American lives in anticipation of the future because he knows it will be a great place. Other people fear the future as just a repetition of past failures. There's a lot of truth in that. If there is one thing we are sure of it is that history need not be relived; that nothing is impossible and that man is capable of improving his circumstances beyond what we are told is fact. After inauguration day, I went to work with a very pointed and specific plan: cut taxes, get control of Federal spending, and get the government out of the way so that the entrepreneurial spirit of the American people could be released. Once people had extra money in their pockets and incentives to invest and build businesses, jobs would be created, inflation reduced, and interest rates reduced. The result – a booming economy and happy Americans.

KENNEDY

Ron, most of the reforms and programs that helped people in the '60's were necessary to bring the United States into the role of leadership in the modern world that we've enjoyed ever since. Those programs really paved the way for millions of people to lead fulfilling lives and not ones of desperation and despair. Of course, in my mind, Jack was one of our greatest presidents but I also personally give a lot of credit to LBJ for following through with what Jack saw for the future of America and eventually everyone in the world. If not for the Vietnam War, LBJ could have gone down in history as one of our best presidents. The war just tore the man apart as it had most of us who were alive at the time.

We saw nightly news broadcasts of body bags containing soldiers. We mourned thousands and thousands of men who were killed and feared for there was no end in sight.

REAGAN

Yes, it was a horrible time in our nation and it took Republicans, Nixon and Ford, to finally end that terrible war.

KENNEDY

It took the anguish and heart and soul and work of many Americans through protest after protest to finally bring that war to its end. Nixon, and later Ford, for the final months of troop withdrawal, had no choice but to end it. The American people saw it as unjust and finally the power of the people stopped it. We honor the brave heroes who fought in that war and those who died and the MIAs. That war changed how Americans thought towards war. It permanently scarred us but I hope it taught lessons as well. Hopefully, future presidents and members of Congress will think twice before committing our troops to battle, to make absolutely sure that the action is truly just and right and that there is a clearly defined exit strategy.

Ron, your presidency had many popular moments but it just dawned on me that you were really, and I'm not trying to be a smart alec about this, just a baby in politics compared to me when you were elected president. I grew up in politics and was senator long before you entered the race for California governor. When you've been around as long as my family and I have in politics, you really get to know how things work inside and out. By the time you came along on the national platform winning elections against Jimmy

Carter and Fritz Mondale, many of the extremely difficult issues of our time were already moving toward reconciliation. The Vietnam War had ended, the Civil Rights Movement had gone through its most difficult period, although far from ending, and Watergate was part of history. However, I remember that the factor of age discrimination came up in your re-election campaign.

REAGAN

That reminds me of the zinger I used during the debate with Walter Mondale before I won my second term. A question was brought up about my age, seventy three at the time, being a factor in governing. My opponent, former Vice President Walter Mondale, of course, was a man of distinction, but still younger than myself. When the commentator asked me if age were a factor in the campaign, it just popped into my head at the right time, and I said, "I will not make age a factor in this campaign. I will not exploit for political purposes my opponent's youth and inexperience".

Ted, your distinguished career is something everyone wants to hear you talk more about. Let's hear about your earlier days.

KENNEDY

After Jack's inauguration and appointing Bobby Attorney General, room was open for me to take over Jack's senate seat. Growing up in a family like mine, I was interested in politics from childhood. While Jack was a Senator he further inspired me. I wanted to go to Law School because that was a way to be effective in public policy- to know the law. First, I completed undergrad at Harvard and then attended University of Virginia Law School at Charlottesville. I really got started in a similar way to you Ron, by going around making speeches for my brother as his Campaign Manager for his 1958 re-election to the Senate. Jack gave me a lot of pointers along the way and really brought me along. Jack won re-election in a huge victory.

Basically, I suppose I learned as I went along by being thrown into the arena as it were. My whole life was like that. Much was expected of me because I was a Kennedy brother. I just grew up with the idea that making speeches was something that was naturally expected of me to do, so I did it.

REAGAN

Ted, you were saying that in your speeches you talked about the important issues of Social Security, Medicare, and Unemployment Insurance. Regarding Social Security, for example, I know that during the height of the great depression FDR knew that something had to be done to help the vast majority of people who, when they reach their "golden years", would not be totally penniless. I also understand that widows and their children and persons with disabilities need help. Those were difficult times and I agree that something had to be done. However, perhaps the program should have been a temporary measure that would have eventually dissolved after the depression era generation passed on and that younger people who were born into a time of new prosperity would not be burdened with having those Social Security taxes involuntarily yanked from their paychecks. Wouldn't it be a better idea to allow young people who are just starting out in life to do what they wish with their own money that they have earned? The federal government should not be involved with grabbing a wage earners dollars and forcing them to invest in a system which may not prove to be as beneficial to them in the long run as if they invested their money on their own in the free marketplace.

KENNEDY
What about the widows and helpless children, and persons with disabilities?

REAGAN
A voluntary fund could be created in the private sector to take care of those persons with special need.

KENNEDY
Ron, I think it's kind of amusing that after all these years we get to have this kind of argument face to face and in front of an audience no less. Your Republican idea of privatization of Social Security would never work. First of all, how can we be sure that everyone would save a sufficient amount of money to be covered in their old age? Secondly, not everyone is well versed in finance and investing. Even the best investments can go "belly up" without warning. Suppose the market crashes? What if people get taken over by unscrupulous investment brokers? People would be left with nothing and there would be no cash reserve to help them. Haven't you Republicans learned that you can't throw the American people to the wolves?

REAGAN
Haven't you Democrats learned that United States Citizens are members of a free society guaranteed by the Constitution and government has no right to shove it's hand into the pockets of wage earners and take money and redistribute those funds as _it_ sees fit to do?

KENNEDY

The great Franklin Delano Roosevelt said that he made Social Security specifically with the provision of a contribution from workers so that, quote, "No Damn politician can ever change it." Having the workers contribution come right out of their paycheck guarantees their right to collect those payments when they need them. Social Security and Medicare are those two programs that have distinguished our nation as a wonderful land where our senior citizens are not left by the wayside having to rely on charity for their daily bread and health.

REAGAN

Since you brought up Medicare, let's look at that one too Ted.   There's another big "government knows best" bureaucracy. Sure, you Democrats meant well. President Lyndon Johnson's Great Society and all that business, but you never stopped to think that Medicare should have never been created because the private sector could have done such a better job of providing health insurance coverage for older Americans. Medicare is another example of forcing Americans to give up their hard earned dollars to "Big Brother" government and be forced to accept the kind of coverage that "Big Brother" wants them to have. If that money were available to the individual who earned it, I'm sure that the open market would provide an insurance company to their liking. The competitive element of the free market would keep costs down. And, by the way Ted, this universal health care system that you've been proposing would amount to the largest government intrusion in personal rights that we've seen yet. You guys never give up!

KENNEDY

That's right Ron. I never give up helping the American people, especially those who can't help themselves.

REAGAN

As I do also as I see fit. But Ted, other than the truly disabled, what's their excuse for not helping themselves? As I stated earlier, there are job opportunities and educational opportunities. Sometimes people must take initiative to work their way up. The pioneers that forged America worked their way up through the sweat of their brow and never gave up. Is the problem that some individuals are more encouraged by the system to look for handouts and have government find their answers? Perhaps some individuals are experiencing psychosocial dysfunction. For some reason they have a mental block. Maybe they don't like this job or that job or it doesn't pay as much as one that they were laid off from. But therein lies the rub, Ted. If someone is truly suffering from emotional or psychological trouble, then they need to see a doctor.

KENNEDY

That's just the problem, Ron; maybe they can't afford to see a doctor! Maybe because they're out of work they have no health insurance coverage and no money to pay a doctor. Or maybe because they're working one of the low wage jobs that you want them to take, they're stuck because their employer can't afford to buy or refuses to buy employee health insurance. Affordable, universal health insurance for all Americans has been one of the most important issues of my entire life.

Come on, admit it Ron, even when you were negotiating nuclear arms limitations with the Soviets, our Democratic social programs helped you. You told me about it yourself Ron. You spoke about the time Gorbechev was telling you about why Communism was better because no one is unemployed under Communism.

REAGAN

Ted, you've tempted me to talk about one of the most fulfilling triumphs of my Presidency. The nudging over of the domino, so to speak, that led to the end of the Soviet Union.

During my first term as President I thought about the idea of rendering nuclear war obsolete. At an assembly with the Chairmen of the Joint Chiefs of Staff I called for the pursuit of the invention of a defensive weapon that could intercept enemy nuclear missiles and destroy them before they got very far after being launched. As the research proceeded, the idea evolved into an outer space based system. There was to be a satellite type defensive grid, so to speak, which would contain interceptors with the means to "zero in" on incoming missiles and blow them to bits before they got very far off the ground. It was given the title SDI or Strategic Defense Initiative.

KENNEDY

Ron, I admit that I was the Member of Congress who gave it the nickname Star Wars and then the press picked up on it. I had gone to see the movie and thought it was a good jab at you. I was against spending billions on yet another weapon and thought that we could come up with an arms limitation treaty without spending billions more dollars and then later having to dismantle it if we came to an agreement.

REAGAN

Your frugality would have been a good thought if it had focused on wasteful government spending, but I contend that SDI, Star Wars as you called it, was the single most important element of our defense policy. It helped make historic breakthroughs in our quest for peace and the eventual fall of the Soviet Union. Our administration's motto became "peace through strength" and it worked. Throughout long and arduous negotiations with the Soviets, they constantly asked for our side to halt research on SDI, as I might add, they took a stab at developing their own. Throughout the process however, as I met with Soviet leader Gorbachev, a wonderful thing was happening. We were becoming friends, and he was beginning to change his way of thinking. In the spring of 1987, Gorbachev had brought about the political movement known as Perestroika and his program of reform called glasnost which opened the Soviet Union up to westernization allowing for some capitalism and democracy. It soon became evident that things were beginning to change for the better in the Soviet Union.

KENNEDY

So Ron, please get to the part where you and my brother have both had the common experience of great speeches in front of the Berlin Wall.

REAGAN

In June of 1987, I accepted an invitation to speak in West Berlin, Germany at the Brandenburg Gate at the dividing line between West and East Berlin near the same place that your brother John spoke so eloquently twenty -seven years earlier. Just as when President Kennedy spoke, thousands of people gathered again. In my speech I mentioned that, "We hear much from Moscow about a new policy of reform and openness. There is one sign the Soviets can make that would be unmistakable, that would advance dramatically the cause of freedom and peace. Then I said: General Secretary Gorbachev, if you seek peace, if you seek prosperity for the Soviet Union and Eastern Europe, if you seek liberalization: come here to this gate! Mr. Gorbachev, open this gate! Mr. Gorbachev, tear down this wall!" Later, not only was an arms limitation treaty signed, the Berlin Wall came down and the Soviet Union was dismantled. Freedom and democracy reigned.

KENNEDY
But please get to the part about when you told Gorbachev about our social programs.

REAGAN
I know you love that part Ted. Okay, well it went like this: When Mikhail Gorbachev and I met in Washington the subject came up about Soviet Jews being allowed to leave the Soviet Union. Gorbachev became slightly indignant, and made it a point to say that the proposal in our country to build a fence along the Mexican border was as bad as anything the Soviets had done with regard to retaining people. I told him that the fence idea was to stop illegal immigration. It was because many Mexicans wanted to become part of our society and enjoy our economic opportunities and democratic system. I explained that it was not the same as the Berlin Wall which kept people in prison in a societal system that was not working for them and that they wanted to escape from. Gorbachev asked, "What about your people who sleep in the streets and all your unemployed? Where are their human rights?" We

have something in this country called unemployment insurance I told him. When a person loses their job, for a certain period of time they continue to collect a payment. Gorbachev asked, "What happens when that certain period of time ends and the person still has no job?" Then there is another program I said, called welfare. If they still can't find a job, then they are eligible for that program.

KENNEDY

See, that's what I was getting at Ron. Without the Democrats and our social programs the Soviets may have proved you wrong on some issues.

REAGAN

Well Ted, I never said that the Democrats ideas were totally bad, but I feel that all of them could be handled far more efficiently being run by the private sector.

KENNEDY

What if the private sector puts profit in front of caring for people in need?

REAGAN

Ted, I guess we'll have to forever agree to disagree.

KENNEDY

Deal.

REAGAN

With that I think its time to start a wrap up.

KENNEDY

Deal again, Ron.

REAGAN
(To audience.)

Always remember that you are Americans, and it is your birthright to dream great dreams in this sweet and blessed land, truly the greatest, freest, strongest nation on earth. I know that for America there will always be a bright dawn ahead. Lastly, as I said as George Gipp in the movie <u>Knute Rockne All American:</u> "Some day when things are tough and the breaks are going against the boys, ask them to go in there and win one for the Gipper. I don't know where I'll be, but I'll know about it and I'll be happy."

KENNEDY

My brother John talked about passing the torch to a new generation.
(To audience.)

I pass it to you: For you and for me, for our country and for our cause and for those whose cares have been our concern…The work begins anew, the hope rises again and the dream lives on! May God bless you all.

REAGAN
(To audience.)

And may God bless the United States of America.
(Both wave, bow and exit.)

END

www.ingramcontent.com/pod-product-compliance
Lightning Source LLC
Chambersburg PA
CBHW070505290526
45790CB00003B/1108